HOW TO

Sleep Tight

THROUGH THE NIGHT

HOW TO
Sleep Tight

THROUGH THE NIGHT

**Bedtime Tricks
(That Really Work!) for Kids**

Tzivia Gover & Lesléa Newman
Illustrated by Vivian Mineker

Storey Publishing

The mission of Storey Publishing is to serve our customers by publishing practical information that encourages personal independence in harmony with the environment.

Edited by Deanna F. Cook and Sarah Guare
Art direction and book design by Carolyn Eckert
Text production by Liseann Karandisecky
Illustrations by © Vivian Mineker

Text © 2022 by Tzivia Gover and Lesléa Newman

Storey Publishing
210 MASS MoCA Way
North Adams, MA 01247
storey.com

Printed in China by Toppan Leefung Printing Ltd.
10 9 8 7 6 5 4 3 2 1

Library of Congress Cataloging-in-Publication Data on file

Storey books are available at special discounts when purchased in bulk for premiums and sales promotions as well as for fund-raising or educational use. Special editions or book excerpts can also be created to specification. For details, please call 800-827-8673, or send an email to sales@storey.com.

For children everywhere—sleep tight!

Let's Go to Sleep!

Some nights, you just don't want to shut out the lights—or shut your eyes—at bedtime because there are still fun things to do.

Or you may be scared of the dark, or worried about having bad dreams.

But you need sleep, even more than grown-ups do. And you need more of it! That's because while you sleep, your body and brain are busy helping you grow. Plus, when you get a good night's sleep, you feel sunnier and more energetic when you wake up.

Luckily, you can get better at sleep, just as you can get better at throwing a ball or playing an instrument. It just takes practice.

Feel good and cozy at bedtime, fall asleep, and become friends with your dreams by following the suggestions in this book. So, turn the page. Before you know it, you'll be ready to turn over and turn off the light.

Make a Night Notebook

Keep a notebook by your bed. You can buy a notebook or make your own by folding and stapling or sewing several pieces of paper together. Use stickers, markers, or crayons to decorate the cover.

On the cover, draw a picture of your favorite stuffed toy, the stars and moon, or an animal friend to help you feel safe and cozy when you pick it up to write or draw.

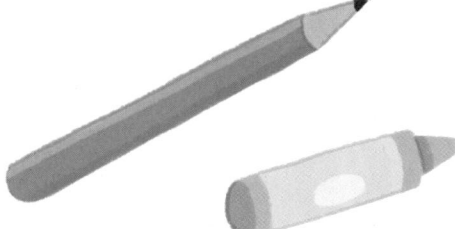

Before you go to sleep, draw or write about your day.

After you wake up, draw or write about your dreams.

Love Your Bed

Some kids can fall asleep in the back seat of the car, or on the couch, but there's one place that's meant just for sleeping: your bed! Sure, you do other things in your room besides sleep, but it's called a bedroom because sleeping in your bed is the most important thing to do there.

What do you love about your bed?

My special pillow

My animals who sleep with me

My cozy blanket

Draw a picture of your cozy bed before you snuggle in and get sleepy!

Swap Plugs for Pages

The hour before bedtime, or after you get into your pajamas, is the time to unplug your electronics.

Trading plugs for pages helps your brain slow down so you can recharge overnight and power up for a new day.

Instead of watching TV or going online, read a book.

Instead of playing a video game, do a puzzle or play a board game.

Add Pizzazz to Your Pillow

Here's a fun way to slip into dreams. Ask a grown-up for a plain pillowcase and permission to decorate it. Find some fabric markers and a piece of cardboard, then let's get started.

* Choose what you want to draw. Think of something that makes you smile: stars, the moon, your favorite animal, or a picture from a dream!

* Practice drawing it on paper.

* Next, place a piece of cardboard inside the pillowcase, so the colors don't run through.

* Using fabric markers, draw your creation on the pillowcase.

* Let the ink dry overnight. Take out the cardboard and wash the pillowcase before putting it on your pillow.

Follow the Milky Way

There are lots of things to do before going to bed, like tidying your room, brushing your teeth, and changing into your pajamas. Those things might seem boring because you do them every night. But there's a fun way to think about your bedtime routine.

Did you know there's **a starry path** through the night sky **called the Milky Way?**

Imagine that as you take each step to get ready for bed, you are **stepping from star to star** on a path that leads into the land of sleep.

Three (or More!) Good Reasons to Go to Bed

It's bedtime, but you want to keep playing. Instead of coming up with reasons why you should stay awake, think of three (or more) reasons why it's really a good idea to go to bed. For example:

1. While you sleep, your body works hard to grow.

2. When you sleep, your brain helps you remember what you learned during the day.

3. Your dreams have a job to do, too. They help you feel calmer and happier.

What are three more—serious or silly—reasons to go to bed?

My hair needs time to grow.

Make Sweet-Smelling Dreams!

The smell of some flowers and plants can relax you. Others help you have more dreams, or better dreams. Mix them up and you can make a dream sock to put under your pillow.

Grab a handful each of three or four of these dried herbs:

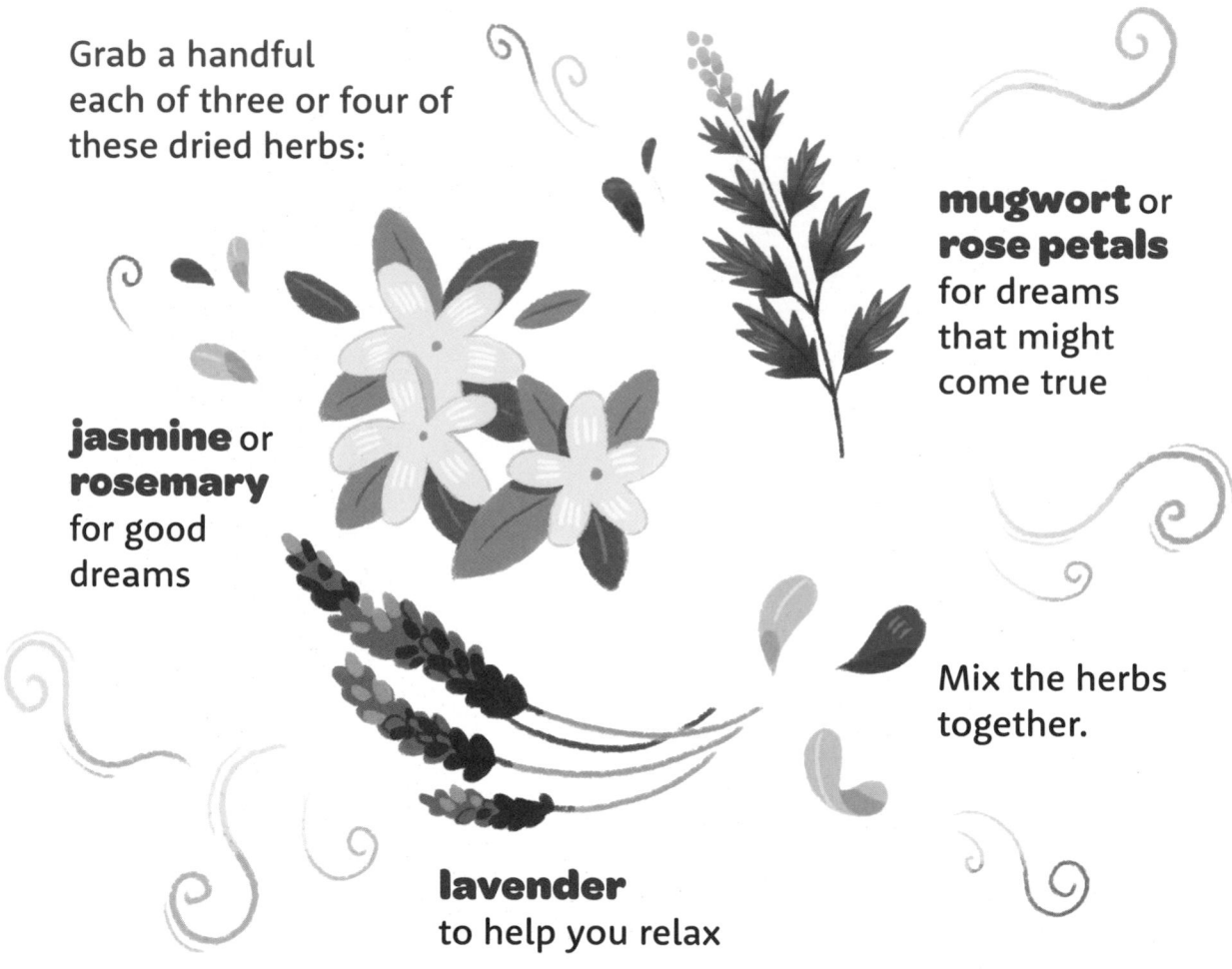

mugwort or **rose petals** for dreams that might come true

jasmine or **rosemary** for good dreams

Mix the herbs together.

lavender to help you relax

Spoon the herbs into a clean sock. Stuff it loosely.

Tie the top of the sock with a tight knot.

For extra softness, add cotton balls in the toe of the sock and on top of the herbs.

sweet dreams

Slip your sock under your pillow or into your pillowcase.

Pitch a Reading Tent

Find a flashlight and gather up your favorite stuffed animal and a book. Crawl into bed and pull the covers up over your head, so you feel like you're inside a tent.

Read in your cozy hiding place for a few minutes, then shut off the flashlight and go to sleep.

Say Thank You

Some people count sheep to fall asleep. But counting the things you feel grateful for works even better. Before bed, make a list or draw pictures of things that made you feel good today. Then, when you're tucked under the covers, close your eyes, imagine each one, and silently say thank you.

Let yourself drift off to sleep with a smile.

Tuck Your Worries in at Night

Everyone worries sometimes. But worrying doesn't fix problems, and it just might keep you awake when you want to sleep.

If something is worrying you, **write it down on a slip of paper** and put it in a small container or box.

You can even decorate the box!

Imagine that a dream helper or fairy is taking care of your worries until morning.

So, instead of worrying, you can get a good night's sleep.

Watch the Stars Fall

Gazing up at the stars in the night sky can make you feel relaxed and sleepy. Whether or not you can see stars outside, you can bring them indoors with this project.

1. Fill a glass jar one-third of the way full with very warm tap water. Add 1 to 3 drops of dark blue food coloring.

2. Add clear school glue until the jar is half full. Whisk until the glue dissolves.

3. Stir in a couple of spoonfuls of glitter (star glitter if you have it!).

4. Fill the jar to the top with more tap water.

5. Put the lid on and twist it until the jar is securely closed.

Make sure your jar has a lid that fits tightly.

water + glitter

clear school glue

water + food coloring

GLUE

Before bed, shake the jar, then watch the stars

drift to the bottom as your thoughts settle down, too.

Climb aboard a Sleep Adventure

Bedtime doesn't have to be boring. When you close your eyes, imagine you are about to take a journey to dreamland. Snuggle under your favorite blanket, then . . .

Pretend your bed is flying through the sky.

Imagine it's a raft that's floating down a river.

Make believe it's a magic train chugging along its tracks.

Climb aboard, close your eyes, and see where your adventure leads you.

Nod Off with Numbers

If you want to sleep but your brain keeps spinning like a top, give your mind some numbers to focus on so you can sink into sleep.

Try counting backward from 10.

If any other thoughts come into your mind, just go back to 10 and try again.

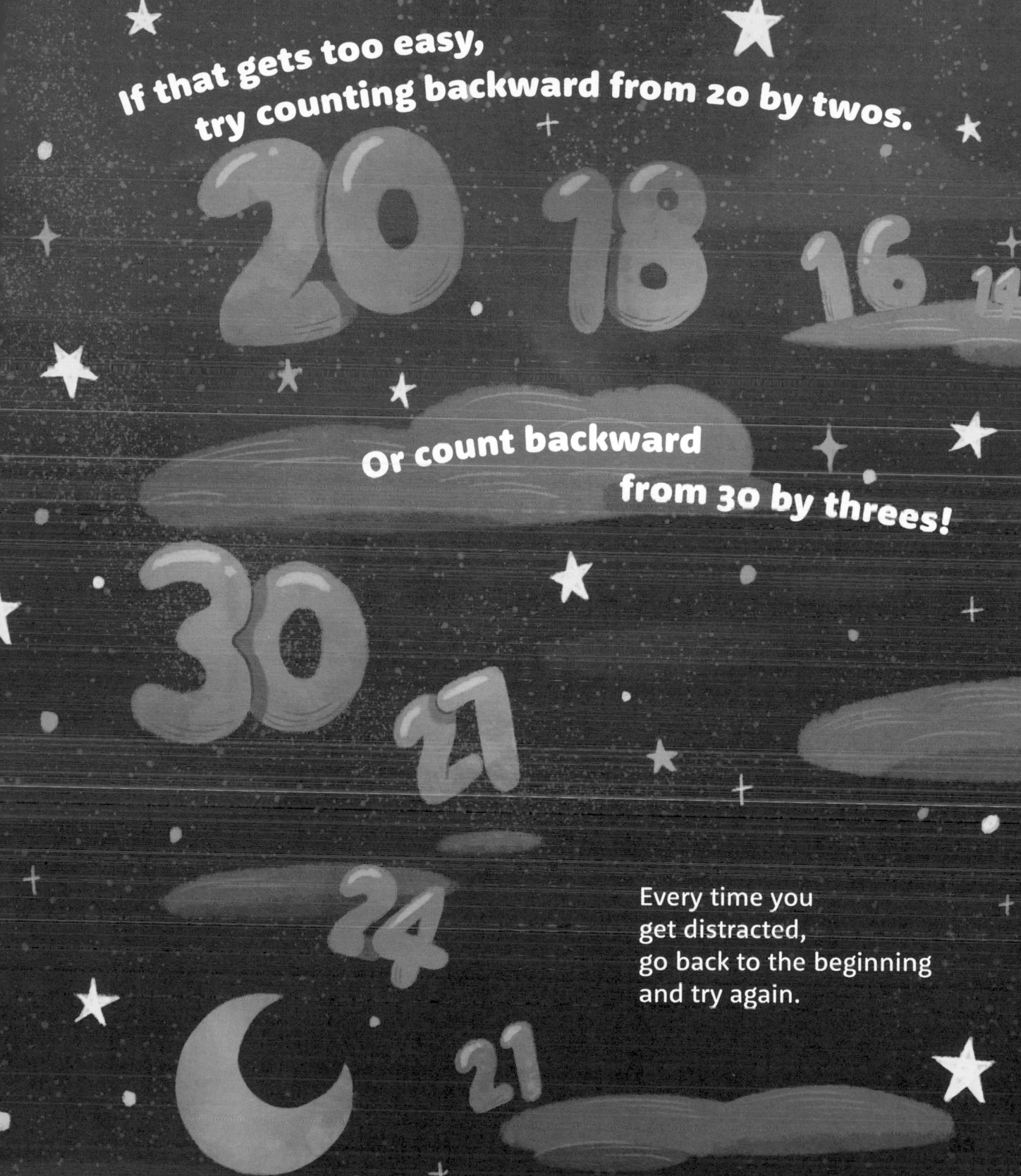

If that gets too easy, try counting backward from 20 by twos.

20 18 16 14

Or count backward from 30 by threes!

30 27 24 21

Every time you get distracted, go back to the beginning and try again.

Dream Power

Do you ever wish you could fly? In dreams you can do this and many other things!

What could you do in a dream that you can't do when you're awake?

Talk to dinosaurs and have them talk back!

HELLO

Walk through walls!

Breathe In, Breathe Out

At bedtime, if you feel fidgety and can't settle down, try this.

Take a big breath in slowly, and silently say to yourself, "I am . . ."

Then breathe out even more slowly, and silently say, "sleepy!"

Slow your words and breath to a turtle's pace and keep going until you fall asleep.

Make a Wish

Wishing on birthday candles is fun, but birthdays only happen once a year. Luckily, there are lots of other times to make wishes, and bedtime is one of them.

Write a wish on a strip of paper

Become a dancer!

Swim with dolphins!

Drive trucks!

and put it under your pillow.

Think of anything you want!

In the morning, watch for any small or big ways that your wish might be coming true.

Think of Words from A to Zzzzz . . .

While you're lying in bed, think of as many words as you can that begin with the letter A. There's apple, aardvark, anteater, and abracadabra!

What else? Next, think of as many words as you can that begin with the letter B. Keep going through the alphabet.

Before you know it, you'll have gone from **A** to **Z**zzzzz and be snoozing away!

Doze Off to Your Dream Movie

When you climb into bed, imagine you are entering an enchanted movie theater. You buy a ticket, but you have no idea what movie you are going to see.

Snuggle in under the covers and close your eyes.

Imagine a curtain opening up to reveal a magical screen.

Then wait for your dream movie to begin.

NOW PLAYING

Sleepwalk in Your Head

If it's hard to find your way to sleep, imagine walking your dog down the block, or walking to a friend's house close by. Picture how you would get there, step by step.

Close your eyes and imagine you are walking down your sidewalk.

Along the way, you might just wander off to sleep!

Scared? Call on Your Superpowers!

Everyone gets scared sometimes. But everyone has superpowers, too. You don't need an invisibility cloak and you don't have to fly through the clouds. You have other strengths to help you face your fears.

What superpowers do you have to face your fears?

Spreader of Joy!

Best Laugh!

World's Greatest Hugger!

Great Helper!

When you feel afraid of the dark,

or if you wake in the night from a scary dream, think of your superpower to help you feel brave when you go back to sleep.

Sing a Sleep Song

The rhythm of a lullaby can rock you to sleep. If no one can sing to you before bed, you can make up your own song.

Put new words to your favorite lullaby:

Sleepy, sleepy little star,

I wonder what your sweet dreams are.

Up above the world so bright,

will you dream of me tonight?

Sleepy, sleepy little star,

I wonder what your sweet dreams are.

Or make up a song with the names of all the people who love you in it.

Or sing about the things that you're looking forward to seeing or doing tomorrow.

Sweet Dreams Jar

What are some things you want to dream about? Write your ideas on small pieces of colorful paper and place them in a glass jar.

Decorate the lid of the jar however you'd like!

underwater adventures

As your jar fills up, it will get more and more colorful.

skating day

see a sloth

Before you go to bed, pick out a slip of paper.

Happy dreaming!

Did any of your ideas appear in your dreams?

Read Your Dreams

Sometimes it's hard to understand dreams. That's because dreams speak a special language that uses pictures instead of just words.

What might your dreams mean?

A bird might mean . . .

you feel as free as a bird.

A rainy day might mean . . .

you feel sad.

A rainbow might mean . . .

you feel happy.

A hissing cat might mean . . .

you feel angry.

A big wave overhead might mean . . .

you feel afraid.

Being lost in the woods might mean . . .

you feel lonely.

Have fun and remember, the only "right" way to read your dreams is the way that feels right to you.

Banish Bad Dreams by Calling out Colors

Everyone has bad dreams sometimes. If you wake up from a nightmare and feel scared, open your eyes and look around your room. What do you see?

Whisper the name of each familiar thing you see, along with its color.

"There's my red lamp."

"There's my pink poster."

"There's my
purple bunny."

Soon you'll realize that you are safe
at home in your very own bed and
there's no need to feel afraid anymore.

Feel Better

Dreams bring up lots of different feelings. But they can be hard to describe. The following four emotions can help describe almost any feeling.

When you wake up from a dream, ask yourself:

Did I feel scared?

Did I feel mad?

**Naming your emotions
helps you talk about what's happening inside you,
so you can feel better.**

Did I feel sad?   **Did I feel glad?**

Make Friends with Monsters

If a mean dog or creepy ghost shows up in your dream, imagine you can shrink it until it fits inside a safe, clear box you can hold in your hand.

Now that it can't hurt you, ask it questions.

What's your name?

What do you want?

What do you need to tell me?

What are you afraid of?

Why are you scaring me?

Introduce your monster to a grown-up, too. Once you get to know this visitor, you'll start to feel stronger and less afraid.

Be a Sleep Scientist

Did you know that almost all animals dream? Scientists study people and animals while they sleep to learn about their dreams and how they sleep. You can, too.

Watch your pet while they sleep.

(If you don't have a pet, you may be able to watch a friend's pet.)

Do their eyelids twitch?

z z z

They might be dreaming.

Do they wag their tail?

z z

Do they purr?

What else can you observe?
Write it down or draw a picture of what you see.

Yawn Big

Yawning doesn't always mean you're tired or bored. A great big yawn in the morning brings oxygen to your brain to help you get ready for the day. Add a stretch when you yawn and wake up your body, too.

Sit tall in bed or stand up.

Place your hands in front of your chest with your elbows sticking out like chicken wings.

Take a big breath and fill your body with air.

Open your arms wide, open your mouth, stretch, and let out a great big yawn!

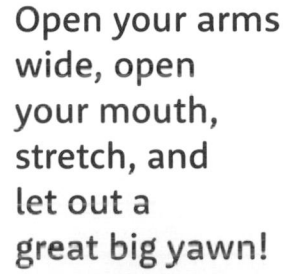

YAAAWWNN

YAAWWNN

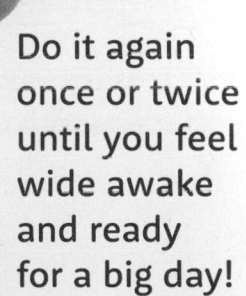

Do it again once or twice until you feel wide awake and ready for a big day!

Discover It Yourself

Inside
The Body

KINGFISHER
LONDON & NEW YORK

KINGFISHER
LONDON & NEW YORK

Published 2022 by Kingfisher
Published in the United States by
Kingfisher, 120 Broadway,
New York, NY 10271
Kingfisher is an imprint of
Macmillan Children's Books,
London
All rights reserved

Copyright © Macmillan Publishers
International Ltd 1995, 2022

Designed by: Tall Tree
Written by: Sally Morgan
Illustrated by: Diego Vaisberg/
Advocate Art

ISBN 978-0-7534-7742-7

First published in 1995 by
Kingfisher
This fully revised and updated
edition published
2022 by Kingfisher

Library of Congress Cataloguing-
in-Publication data has been
applied for.

Kingfisher books are available for
special promotions and
premiums. For details contact:
Special Markets Department,
Macmillan, 120 Broadway, New
York, NY 1027

Printed in China
9 8 7 6 5 4 3 2 1
1TR/1121/WKT/128MA

Contents

Make sure you have a grown-up to help whenever you see this sign.

What Are We Made Of?

Your body is two thirds water. The rest is made up of about 50 billion tiny cells—the basic building blocks of life—which vary in shape and size and carry out different jobs. For example, red blood cells carry oxygen and nerve cells pass messages to and from the brain. Cells have only a limited lifetime, so they have to be repaired or replaced when they wear out. Groups of the same type of cell form body tissues, such as skin and muscle. Groups of different types of tissue make up organs, such as the heart and the lungs. Each organ has a particular job to do in the body.

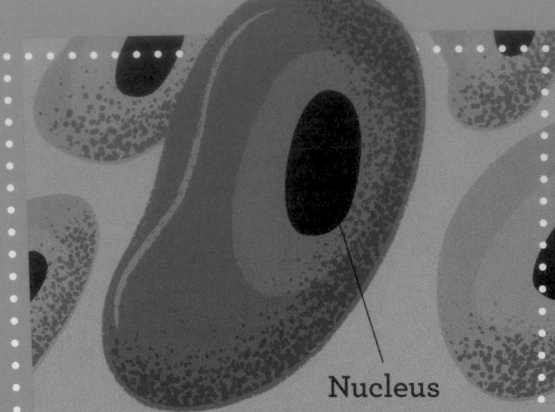

Nucleus

Millions of Cells

Cells cannot be seen with the naked eye, but can be examined under a microscope. They have a membrane around the outside and contain a nucleus, or control center.

Mammals

Humans, like mice, belong to a group of animals called mammals. They share several similar characteristics. They have mammary glands so the females can produce milk for their young, a constant body temperature, which for humans is 98.6°F (37°C), and their skin is covered in hair.

Skeletal muscles are attached to bones. When a muscle shortens, it pulls on the bone and moves it. Muscles also make up your heart and surround your gut.

Your skeleton supports and protects your organs. It is made from bone and cartilage.

Skin covers your body and protects the soft tissue beneath from injury. It also acts as a barrier to microbes that cause disease.

Your brain coordinates and controls your actions.

The food that you eat is broken down and absorbed through the walls of the gut. The food is turned into fuel for your body.

Your heart pumps blood to all parts of your body. Blood carries oxygen, which is needed by every cell.

How tall?

People are taller today than they were 100 years ago. The tallest person ever grew to be 8ft 11.1 inches (272 cm).

How old?

The life expectancy of humans is increasing all the time due to advances in science. The oldest person ever lived to the age of 122.

The Skeleton

The skeleton is the hardest and strongest part of your body. Without it, you could not stand up or move. The skeleton protects your organs, and the muscles that move your limbs are attached to it. The spine supports your body. It is made up of a column of small bones called vertebrae, separated by small rubbery discs of cartilage. These cushion the bones and allow the spine to bend. Joints allow other bones to move.

Skull

Radius

Humerus

Ulna

Shoulder blade

Collar bone

Sternum

Fingers

Ribs

Spine

Hip

Femur

X-rays

Break in arm

The human skeleton is made up of 206 bones. The largest are the thigh bones, or femurs. The smallest are the three tiny bones in the ear.

Doctors use X-rays to take photographs of bones inside a patient's body. This X-ray shows a broken arm.

Fibula

Kneecap

Tibia

Toes

6

DISCOVER IT YOURSELF!

Muscles work in pairs. One contracts, or shortens, while the other relaxes, or stretches.

1. Take two lengths of wood. Ask an adult to help you join the ends using a hinge. This will be an elbow.

2. Carefully attach four hooks to the wood in the positions shown. Use short lengths of string to attach rubber bands between the hooks.

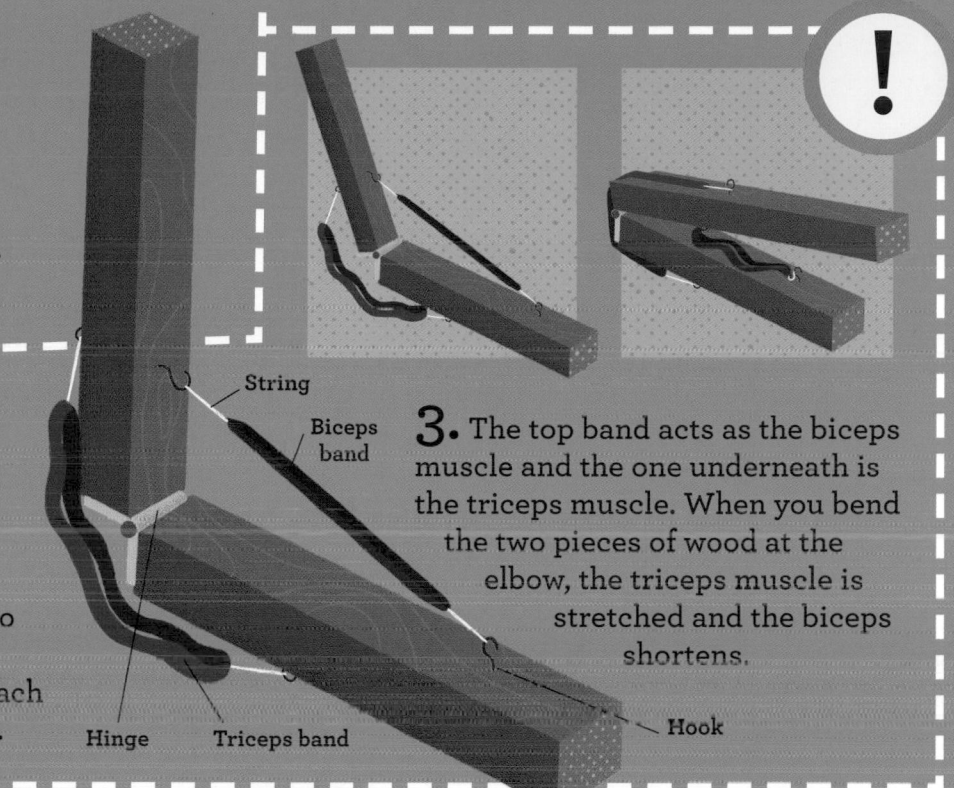

String

Biceps band

Hinge

Triceps band

Hook

3. The top band acts as the biceps muscle and the one underneath is the triceps muscle. When you bend the two pieces of wood at the elbow, the triceps muscle is stretched and the biceps shortens.

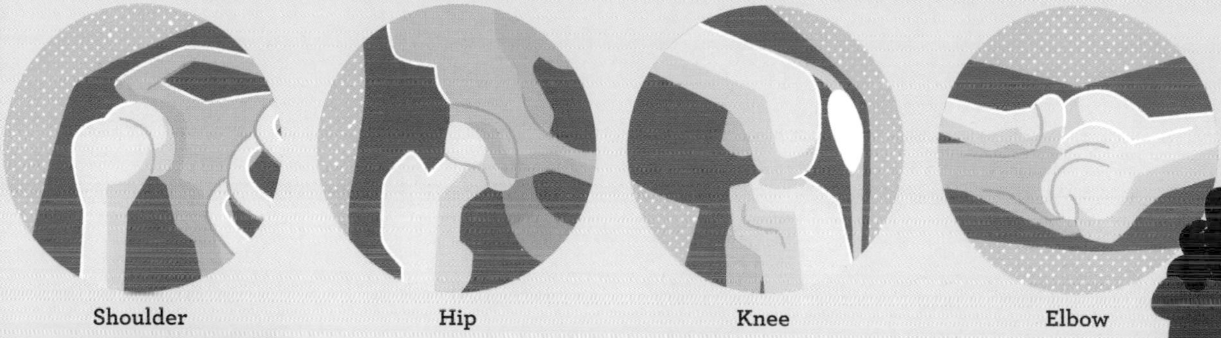

Shoulder   Hip   Knee   Elbow

Joints

Shoulder and hip joints are called ball and socket joints because the upper arm bone and the thigh bone end in a smooth ball that swivels in a hollow socket. This type of joint allows movement in all directions. Elbow and knee joints are called hinge joints because they work like the hinge in a door. These joints move only in one direction, and back again. The bones of a joint are held in place by stretchy ligaments. A smooth layer of cartilage over the ends of the bones acts as a cushion against shock and stops bones from wearing away as they rub against each other.

Teeth

The first set of 20 teeth, called baby teeth, start to appear within a few months of birth. Under the baby teeth, deep in the gums, are the permanent teeth. The first permanent teeth appear at about six years of age. They push out the baby teeth as they grow. An adult has 32 teeth. Beneath the tough outer covering of enamel is dentine, which makes up most of the tooth. It is softer than enamel and is easily damaged by decay. Deep in the middle is the pulp cavity, which contains nerves and blood vessels.

Incisors and Molars

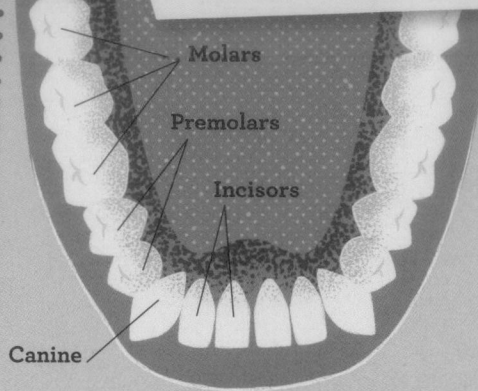

The sharp incisors at the front are for biting food, and the canines next to them are for tearing food. Premolars and molars are large, flat teeth at the back that are used for chewing food.

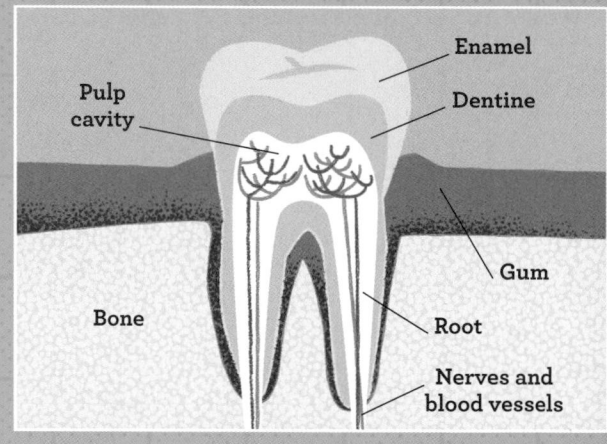

A colorless, sticky layer called plaque forms over your teeth. Unless you brush your teeth properly, it hardens to form tartar, a tough layer that is difficult to remove and eventually leads to gum disease and tooth decay.

Avoid Teeth Like These!

Bacteria in your mouth produce acids that dissolve away the surface of the tooth's enamel and cause dental decay. Toothache starts when decay reaches the nerve. A dentist will remove the decay and replace it with a filling made of metal or a white plastic material that blends in better with the tooth.

DISCOVER IT YOURSELF!

Some teeth are designed to bite off food, and others are better for chewing. The teeth you use to bite off food have sharp edges. Those for chewing are larger with a flat, ridged surface.

1. Using a mirror, take a good look at the teeth in your mouth. How many teeth do you have? Are they baby teeth or permanent teeth? Can you name them?

2. Bite off a piece of raw carrot and chew it. Which teeth did you use to bite off a piece? Which teeth did you use to chew the carrot? Did your tongue help?

Eye Spy

How many of your teeth have fillings? Carry out a survey to find out how many fillings your friends have. Which teeth are most usually filled? Do your parents have more or fewer fillings than you?

A Healthy Diet

Your body needs a mixture of foods that contain different nutrients. Carbohydrates and fats produce energy. Bread, potatoes, and cereals are rich in carbohydrates. Dairy, oils, and meat contain fat. You need protein for growth and to repair cells. Meat, eggs, and beans provide protein. Your body also needs minerals and vitamins. Calcium helps build strong teeth and bones. Iron, which is needed for red blood cells, can be found in many of vegetables and is added to breakfast cereals.

Vitamins

Vitamins are named by letters. Vegetables and fruit are good sources of Vitamin C. Milk and cheese provide vitamin A. Rice, cereals, and brown bread provide Vitamin B.

What do you eat for breakfast? Most likely, you have a bowl of healthy cereal or oatmeal, and perhaps some toast? Somebody living in Indonesia might have rice mixed with vegetables and topped with an egg. Both meals are a healthy start to the day.

DISCOVER IT YOURSELF!

Try this test to identify foods that contain starch, a carbohydrate found in plant foods.

!

You may have to try this experiment at school.

1. Collect a selection of foods such as a cracker, an apple, cheese, and a potato. Grind up a small sample of one of them.

2. Add a small amount of water and mix well. Leave aside for a few minutes and then pour the liquid into a small container.

3. Add a drop of iodine. If starch is present, the liquid will turn a blue-black color.

4. Repeat this for each food. Which ones contain starch?

Vegetarians and Vegans

People who eat a vegetarian or vegan diet do not eat meat. Their meals are based on vegetables, especially pulses (beans and peas). Vegetarians may have small amounts of eggs, milk, and cheese for protein.

Junk Food

Sweetened drinks, potato chips, hamburgers, and fries are called "junk food" because they are convenient and cheap, but not very healthy. They contain a lot of fat and carbohydrate.

Eye Spy

Look for the list of contents on packaged foods. There may be numbers for energy (calories), fat, and protein, as well as other nutrients. Compare which foods in your home have more of which nutrients.

Digestion

Food provides energy for your body and helps you to grow. When you swallow, chewed food mixed with saliva passes to your stomach and intestines. Digestive juices, which contain chemicals called enzymes, break down the food so that it can pass through the walls of the intestine into the blood system. All that is left once digestion is complete is a small quantity of feces. This contains the bits of food you cannot digest, and it passes out of your body when you go to the toilet.

Salivation

When we see, smell, or think about food, glands under the tongue start to release saliva. This helps to break down food for the digestive process. Animals salivate, too. You may have seen a dog drool when it is given some food.

DISCOVER IT YOURSELF!

Saliva lubricates food so that it is easy to swallow.

1. Chew a small cube of dry bread without swallowing.

2. As the bread becomes mushy, you should start to detect a sweet taste in your mouth.

3. Repeat this with a piece of apple or cheese. Is there any difference?

? How It Works

The enzymes in your saliva break down starch into sugar. This produces the sweet taste in your mouth. This only happens with foods such as bread, which contain cooked starch.

Your digestive system is about 30 feet (9 meters) long. Food passes from your mouth to your stomach, where it is stored for up to four hours. Food may take several days to pass right through the digestive system. Muscles in the walls of the intestines squeeze to push the food along.

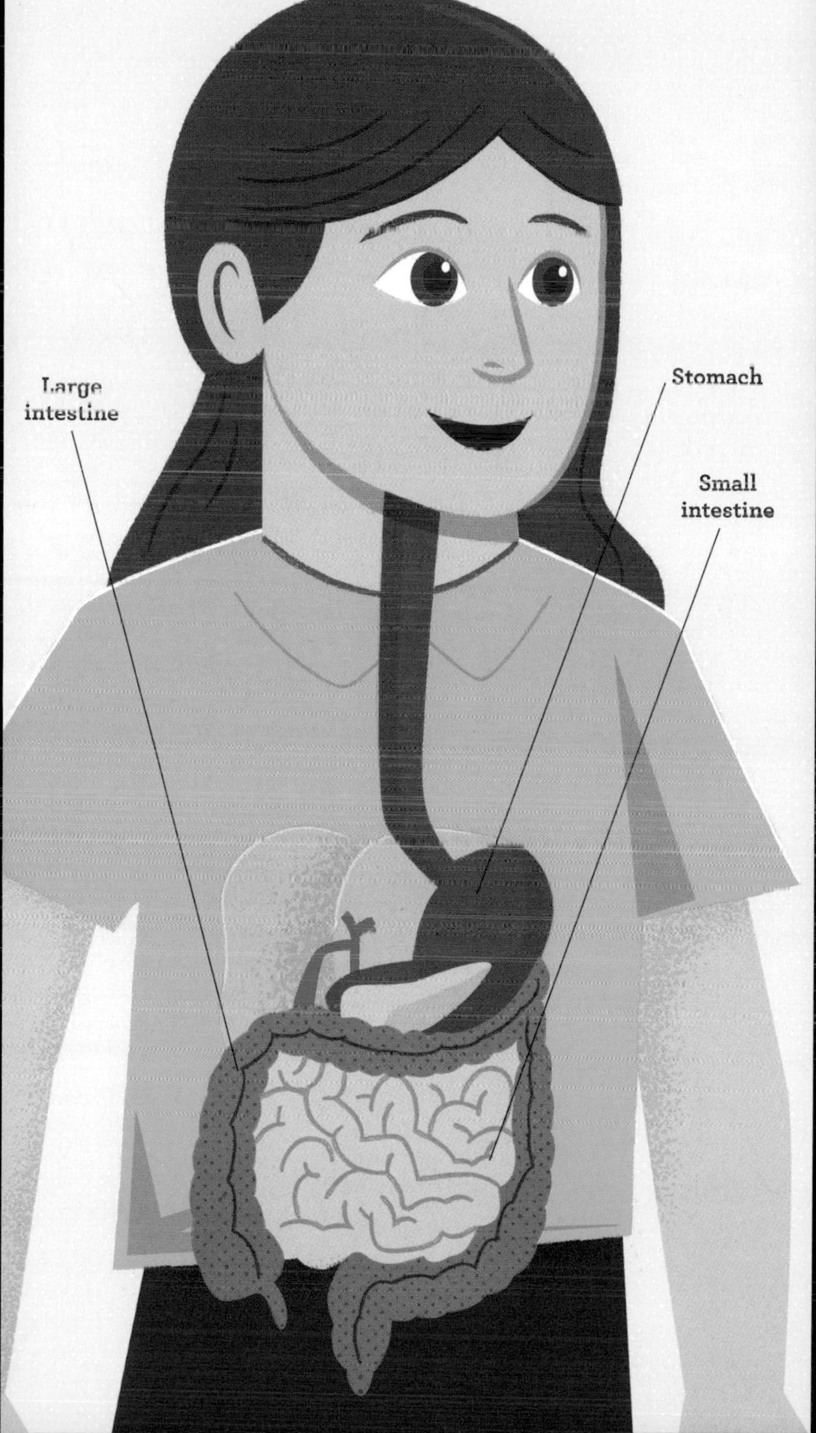

Large intestine

Stomach

Small intestine

Eye Spy

Food provides energy for daily activities, such as walking and running. Make a list of all the things you do during the day that require your body to use energy.

Special Stomachs

Plants contain a tough material called cellulose, which cannot be digested by humans. A cow's large stomach contains bacteria that can digest cellulose. To help digestion, the cow brings up the food and chews it a second time.

The Waterworks

Your kidneys filter out waste and excess water from your blood after food has been digested. The waste materials become a liquid called urine. Urine travels down two tubes called ureters to your bladder, where it is stored. When the sphincter muscle on your bladder relaxes, the urine flows down another tube called the urethra and out of your body. Your kidneys also help you to control the amount of fluid in your body. If you drink a lot of water, your body has to get rid of some, so it produces extra urine.

Hot and Thirsty

During exercise, your skin sweats to help keep you cool. This water has to be replaced, so your brain tells you that you need water by making you feel thirsty.

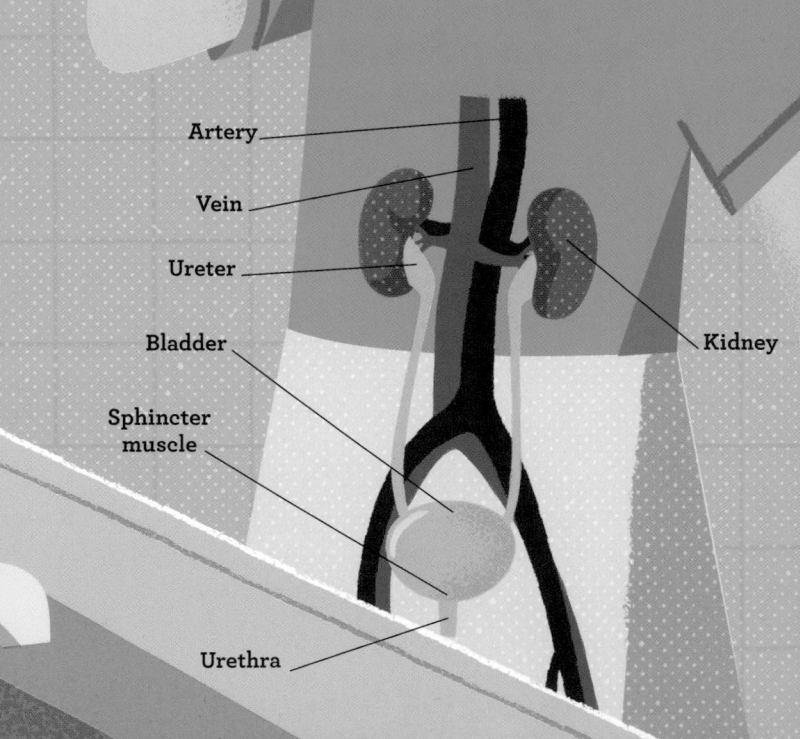

Artery

Vein

Ureter

Bladder

Sphincter muscle

Kidney

Urethra

DISCOVER IT YOURSELF!

You can make a very simple filter to show how a kidney works.

1. Fold a piece of paper towel into a cone shape to make a filter. Put the filter into a plastic funnel. Place the funnel in a container.

2. Grind up some chalk and mix the powder in water so that it is very cloudy. Pour the cloudy water into the filter.

3. The water that drips from the filter is much clearer than the water that went into the filter. The filter in your kidney is similar. It lets some of the water and all of the waste through, but keeps back the valuable blood cells.

Why Do Babies Need Diapers?

Babies have no control over the moment when urine passes out of their bladder. They have to learn how to use the sphincter muscle.

Water to Drink

A person can survive for many days without food, but will die within three days without water. In some parts of the world where it is hot and there is not much rain, people sometimes have to travel long distances to find enough clean water to drink. During a severe drought, many people may die.

Heart and Circulation

Blood is circulated all around your body through a system of blood vessels. At the center of the blood system is your heart—pumping tirelessly day and night. Arteries carry blood from your heart to all parts of your body. Veins bring blood back to your heart. Blood carries oxygen from the lungs and food from the intestines to the cells, and picks up carbon dioxide and other waste materials from the cells.

Blood Cells

Blood is made up of plasma and blood cells. Red cells carry oxygen and white cells protect your body from disease.

DISCOVER IT YOURSELF!

Your pulse tells how fast your heart is beating.

1. Take your pulse while you are resting. Count the number of beats you can feel in one minute.

2. Now run up and down some stairs.

3. Take your pulse again. By how much has your pulse rate increased?

? How It Works

When you exercise, your muscles need oxygen. Your heart beats more quickly in order to pump blood to the muscles. Your pulse may increase from 60–75 beats to over 100 per minute.

4. Wait five minutes and measure your pulse again. Has it returned to normal?

The Heart

Your heart is two pumps working side by side. Blood from your body enters the right side and is pumped to the lungs. Blood from the lungs returns to the left side and is pumped to your body.

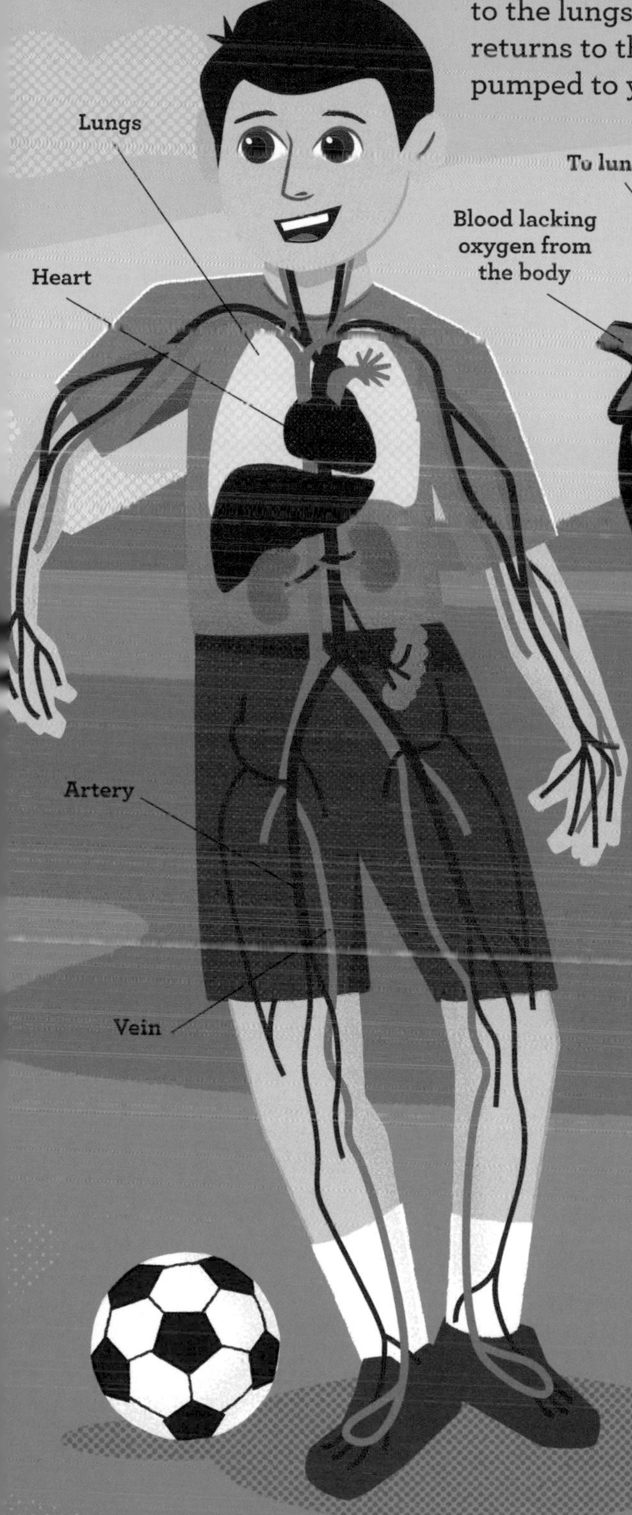

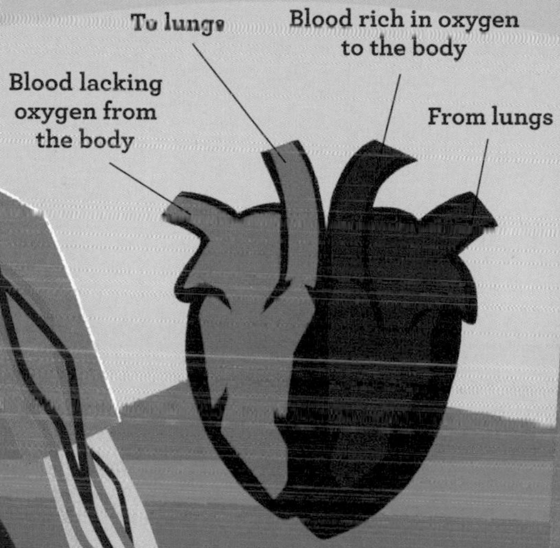

Lungs

Heart

To lungs

Blood lacking oxygen from the body

Blood rich in oxygen to the body

From lungs

Artery

Vein

Your body has 62,000 miles (100,000 km) of blood vessels containing more than 1 gallon (3.8 liters) of blood. Arteries and veins are linked by tiny capillaries.

Blocked Arteries

If arteries in the heart become clogged with fatty deposits, the flow of blood is reduced and part of the heart muscle may not get enough oxygen. The result is often a heart attack.

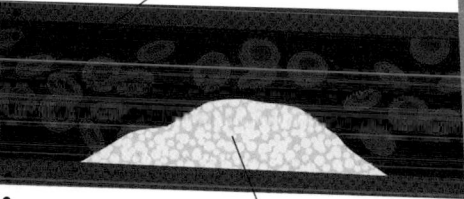

Blood

Fatty deposits

Clotting Blood

Platelets

Red blood cells

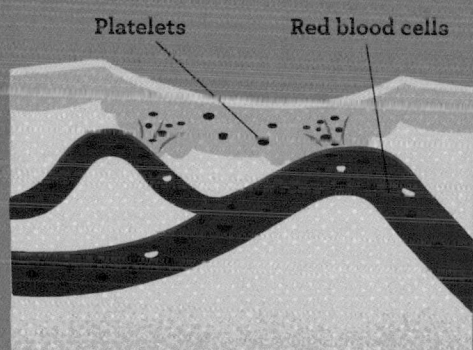

If you cut yourself, small cells in your blood called platelets form a network of fibers across the cut. Red blood cells become trapped in the net and harden to form a scab.

17

Breathing

Every four or five seconds, you take a fresh breath of air into your lungs. When you breathe in, your chest expands as your lungs fill with air. Air contains oxygen, which the blood cells need to release the energy locked up in food. The cells produce a waste gas called carbon dioxide. This is picked up by the blood and carried back to your lungs. When you breathe out, the air that leaves your lungs contains much less oxygen, but an increased amount of carbon dioxide.

The trachea leads from the back of the throat into the chest, and then divides into two narrower tubes called bronchi. These carry air into the lungs. Beneath the lungs there is a muscle called the diaphragm, which moves down when you breathe in, helping to suck air into the lungs, and up when you breathe out again.

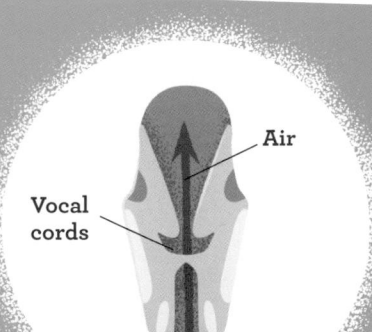

Air

Vocal cords

Voice Box

When you speak, muscles bring your vocal cords close together so that air leaving your lungs is forced through a narrow slit. As air rushes through the cords, they vibrate to produce a sound.

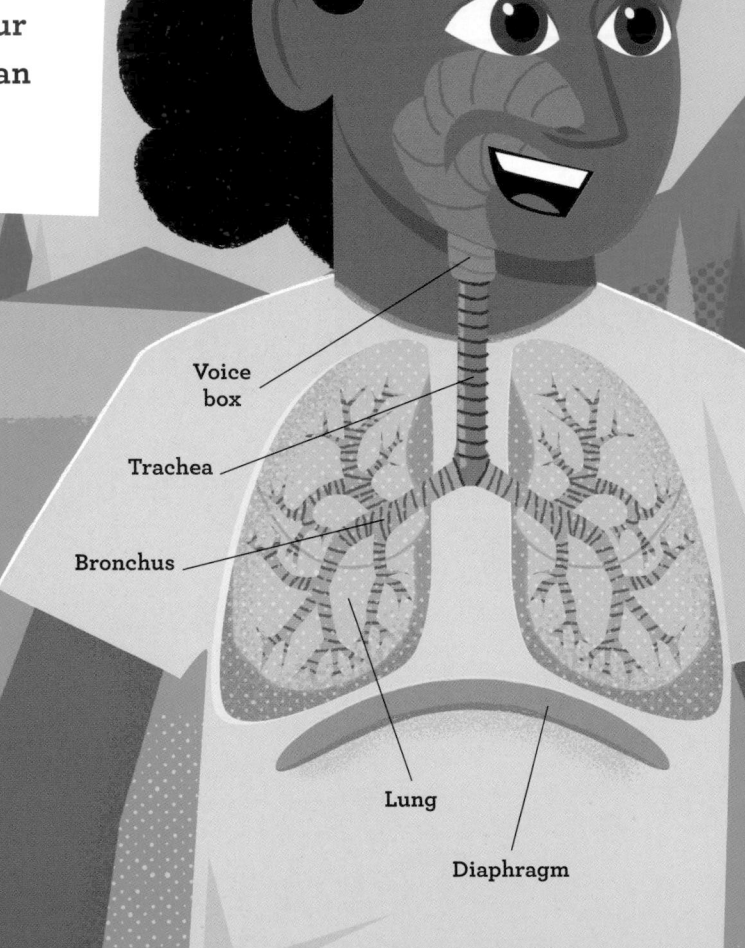

Voice box

Trachea

Bronchus

Lung

Diaphragm

Breathing Under Water

Divers take compressed air with them in a special cylinder. They use a mask and breathing apparatus so that they can breathe normally.

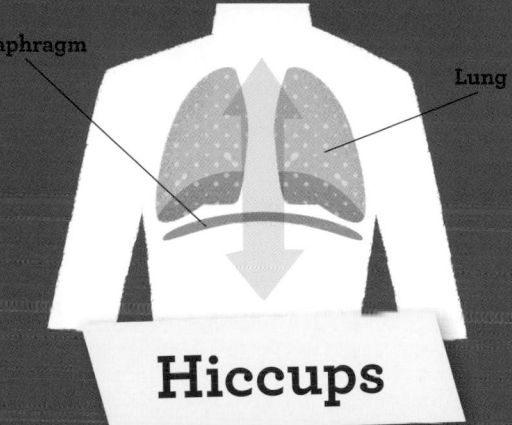

Diaphragm

Lung

Hiccups

Hiccups are caused when your diaphragm contracts sharply. This stops you breathing in normally and your vocal cords make the familiar "hic" sound.

DISCOVER IT YOURSELF!

How much air can you expel from your lungs?

1. You will need a large plastic container, rubber tubing, and a crayon. Fill the container with water.

2. Fill a sink with water and lower the container into the sink. Quickly turn it upside down without letting in any air. Push one end of the rubber tubing into the container, holding your finger over the other end to block it.

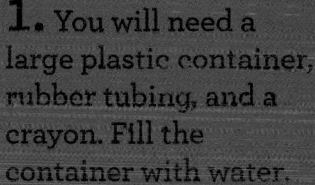

3. Take a deep breath and blow out through the tubing. Mark on the container the water level after you breathed out.

4. Empty the container and then fill it with water up to the mark. This represents the volume of air that you expelled from your lungs.

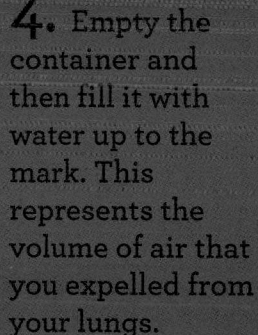

The Nervous System

Your brain is the control center of your body. Without it, you could not move, think, or remember anything. Your brain receives information from all over your body, especially from the senses. It uses this information to coordinate your actions. The nerves carry messages from your brain to all parts of your body. The information kept in your brain for future reference is called memory. This is a store of all the things you have seen, heard, and done.

The brain and spinal cord make up the central nervous system. Nerves then branch off to the rest of the body. This outer network of nerves is called the peripheral nervous system.

Brain

Spinal cord

Peripheral nervous system

Eye Spy

Your brain determines whether you use your right or left hand for writing. Most people are right-handed, but may use the left hand for certain jobs. See which hand you use to do a variety of tasks.

Try this test to see how fast your reflexes are.

1. Sit down with your friend standing in front of you, holding a ruler vertically by its end.

2. Hold your hand open immediately below the ruler, ready to catch it when it drops. Your friend should let the ruler drop without warning.

3. Grab the ruler as it falls through your open hand. Note how far the ruler has fallen by looking at the scale.

4. Try catching the ruler first with the right hand, and then with the left hand.

Reflexes

Some nerves work without the brain being involved. The message rushes along the nerve to the spinal cord and the reply returns along another nerve, telling the muscle to contract. If you sit with one leg crossed over the other and somebody taps your leg just below the kneecap, the lower part of your leg kicks up. This automatic response is called a reflex.

The Brain

The brain is a soft gray organ with a wrinkled surface, protected by the skull. It weighs about 3.3 pounds (1.5 kg) and contains as many as 10,000 million nerve cells. The spinal cord leads down from the base of the brain.

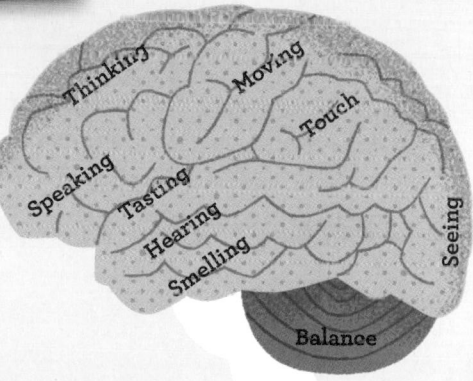

Thinking

Moving

Touch

Speaking

Tasting

Hearing

Smelling

Seeing

Balance

Spinal cord

The Senses

The sense organs turn a stimulus, such as a touch or a noise, into an electrical message that is sent along sensory nerves to your brain. Your skin has nerve endings that are sensitive to pressure, touch, heat, and pain. Your sense of taste comes from taste buds in the mouth. It is linked to the sense of smell, which comes from sensors in your nose. Your ears collect sound waves that enter the ear and hit the eardrum. You see with your eyes. Light rays enter the front of the eye and produce a picture on the retina at the back. The picture is detected by special sensors called rods and cones.

Balance

Ears help you to keep your balance. Inside your ears there are three tubes filled with fluid. When you move your head, the fluid moves and this sends information to your brain.

DISCOVER IT YOURSELF!

See what happens if you eat food without being able to see or smell it.

Apple

Potato

White bread

Cheese

Blindfold a friend. Hold a piece of onion under their nose to dull their sense of smell. Now give them some food to eat. Can they tell you what they are eating?

DISCOVER IT YOURSELF!

You can see some colors out of the corner of your eye more easily.

1. Ask a friend to sit on a stool. Stand behind them. Take two pens of the same color, and hold one in each hand. Put your arms out to the side, at your friend's eye level. Slowly move your arms forward, around the front of your friend.

2. Ask your friend to tell you the color of the pens while keeping their eyes looking to the front.

3. Try with two more pens of a different color. Which color does your friend see out of the corner of their eye more easily?

? How It Works

Bright colors are more easily seen out of the corner of the eye. This is why emergency vehicles use red, blue, and yellow—it helps us to see them coming up behind us.

When you play ball games, your senses are very important. You have to watch the ball and the other players. You have to listen for calls and be ready to move quickly.

Braille

Braille is a form of writing using raised dots. A blind person can feel the dots with their fingertips and translate them into words.

The Skin

Skin provides a protective covering over your bones and muscles. It keeps out bacteria and helps to control your body temperature. The outer layer of skin, the epidermis, is made up of cells. The top cells are dead, and are continually shed to be replaced by new ones from below. The epidermis protects the underlying dermis from the Sun. The dermis contains many nerve endings, blood vessels, and sweat glands. Hairs grow from roots deep in the dermis.

Pigment

Skin tries to protect itself from the sun's rays by producing a dark brown pigment called melanin. People with darker skin have more melanin than those with lighter skin. But everyone should also use protective sunscreen.

Nails

Nails are made from tough fibers of keratin. Fingernails grow about 0.02 inches (0.5 mm) each week. If they are not cut they may grow very long.

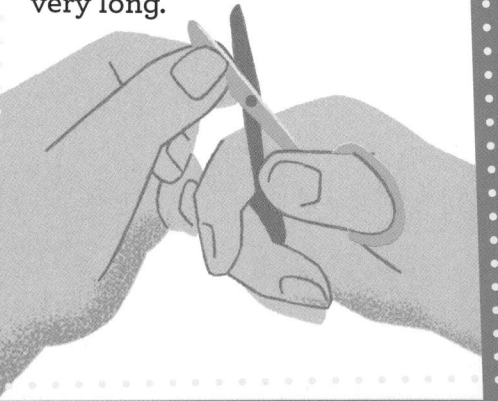

DISCOVER IT YOURSELF!

Fingertips have hot and cold sensors that help you to feel the temperature.

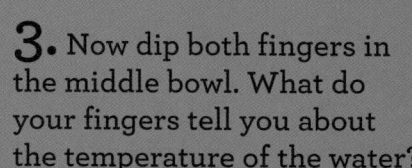

1. Put warm water in one bowl, cool water in another, and ice cold water in the third.

2. Dip one finger in the warm water and one in the ice cold water. Wait for a minute. Can you tell the difference?

3. Now dip both fingers in the middle bowl. What do your fingers tell you about the temperature of the water?

When you come out of a swimming pool, the water evaporates from your skin and this makes you feel cold. The hairs on your skin stand up and you get tiny goose pimples. This helps to trap a layer of warm air around the body and makes it more difficult for heat to be lost.

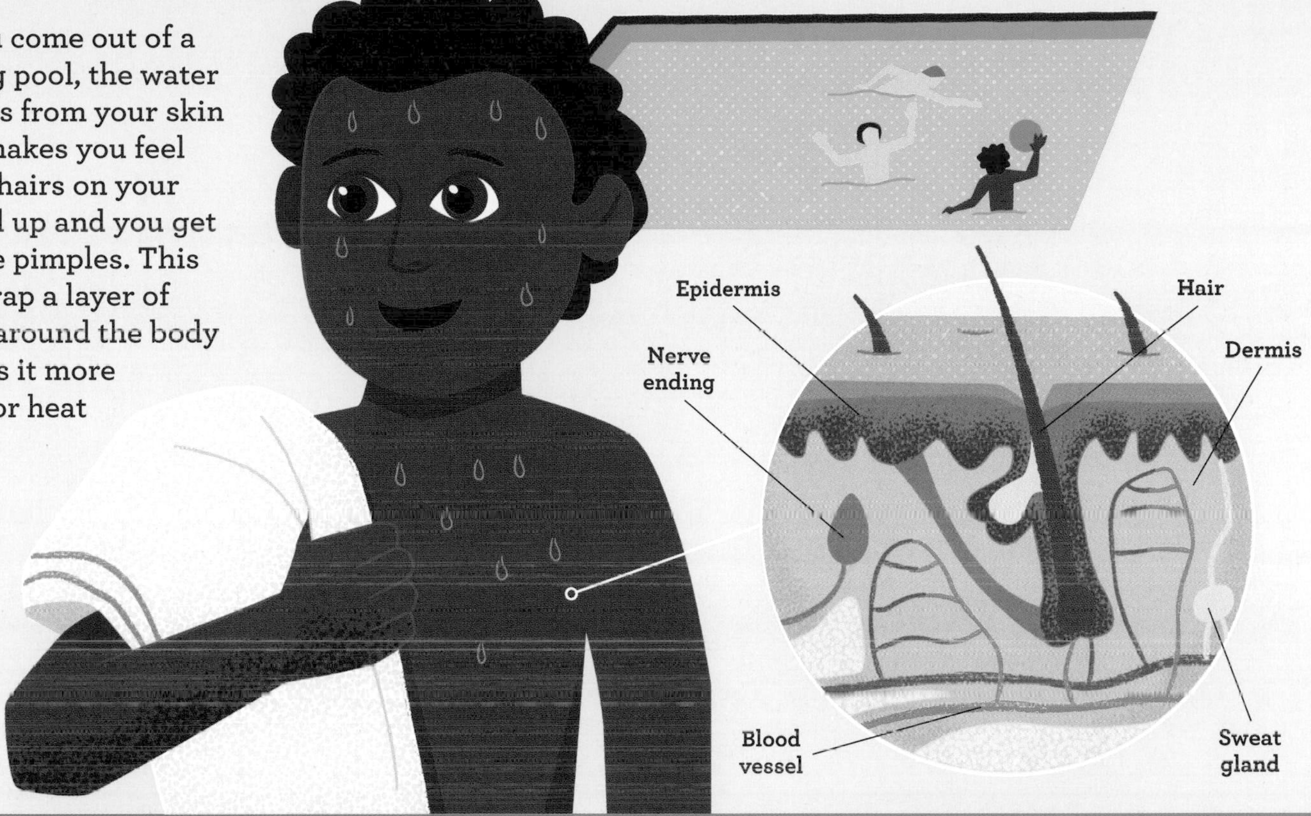

Epidermis

Hair

Nerve ending

Dermis

Blood vessel

Sweat gland

? How It Works

When you moved your fingers into the cool bowl, your brain took a few seconds to notice that the message about temperature had changed.

Fingerprints

Fingerprints are often used to identify people because each person's print is a unique pattern of spirals and whirls. You can take your own fingerprints by pressing your fingertips on an ink pad, then onto a piece of paper.

Inheritance

There are many physical differences between individual people, even if they are of a similar age.

Human beings vary in height, size, hair color, and eye color. Most of your appearance is inherited from your parents. Inherited characteristics are controlled by genetic instructions, or genes. Genes are carried on chromosomes that are found in the nucleus of every cell. Most cells contain two sets of genes. One set of genes is passed from each parent to their child during reproduction. This means that you received one set of genes from your mother and one set from your father, giving you two sets of genes of your own.

Genes

Each of your parents gives you one gene for eye color. If both give you a blue eye gene, you will have blue eyes. If both give you a brown eye gene, then your eyes will be brown. But if one parent gives you a blue gene and the other a brown gene, you will have brown eyes. This is because the gene for brown eyes is stronger than the gene for blue eyes.

DISCOVER IT YOURSELF!

Your classmates vary in height, even though they are all the same age.

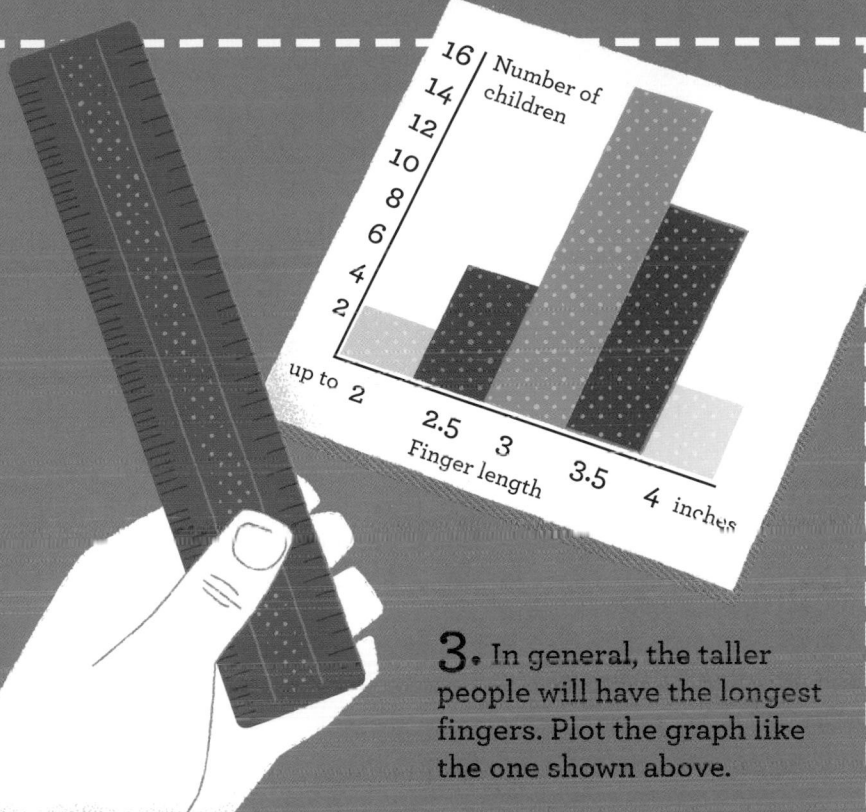

1. Measure your longest finger. Try to measure to the point where the finger stops, rather than to the end of the fingernail.

2. Now measure the length of the same finger on the other people in your class, making sure that you measure to the same point on all your fingers.

3. In general, the taller people will have the longest fingers. Plot the graph like the one shown above.

Identical Twins

Identical twins are produced when a newly fertilized egg divides into two. Instead of one baby developing inside the mother's womb, two babies develop. Because they were formed from the same egg, they carry the same genes and are identical in every way.

Growing Up

The food that you eat helps you to grow. The speed at which you grow depends on glands in the body. These glands make hormones that control the rate at which you use food. People do not grow steadily all the time. A baby grows rapidly, then the rate of growth slows down. It speeds up again between the ages of 11 and 14. Most people stop growing when they are about 20 years old.

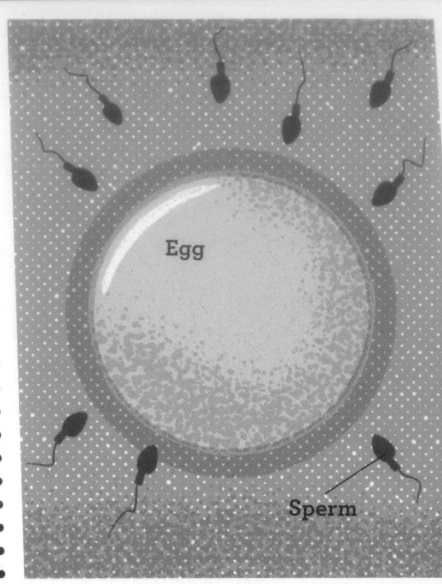

Egg

Sperm

Eye Spy

As people grow older, their bodies change. Old people have wrinkled skin and their limbs are stiffer. What other differences do you notice between a young and an old person?

The Beginning of You

You started life as a tiny fertilized cell. A sperm from your father joined up with an egg in your mother's womb. The fertilized egg then started to divide and your body organs began to form. After three months, you began to look like a miniature baby and to make your first movements. After nine months, you were fully formed and ready to be born.

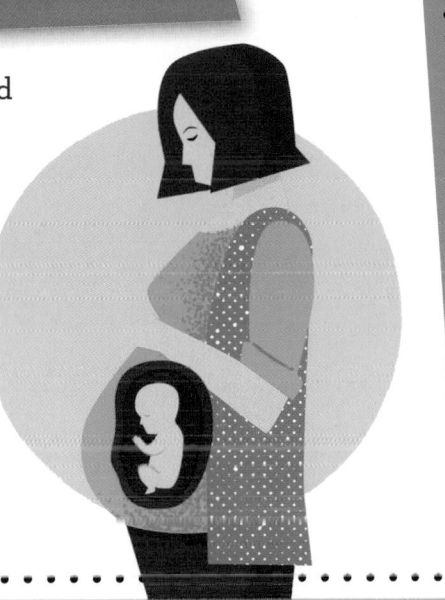

Learning with Age

A newborn baby cannot walk, talk, or read. In the first years of life, a child learns to do all these things.

One significant feature of life is the ability to reproduce, or have babies. People are able to reproduce once they have reached their full size and are mature.

Keeping Fit

When you are fit, your body works well and you feel good. You are more energetic and less likely to suffer from illnesses such as colds or flu. Exercise keeps your muscles firm and strengthens your heart and lungs. To stay fit your body needs plenty of exercise each day. Walking, swimming, cycling, and playing sports are all good exercise. When you exercise, you use up more energy, so it is important to eat a good balanced diet.

Sleep

Getting enough sleep is essential for staying fit. When you sleep, your heartbeat and breathing slow down and your muscles relax.

Eye Spy

There are many things you can do during the day to improve your fitness, such as walking to school and taking the stairs rather than the elevator. How many other things can you think of?

Unhealthy Lifestyle

Eating junk food and spending hours sitting in front of the television is bad for your health.

Healthy Lifestyle

Eating plenty of fresh fruit and vegetables and exercising regularly is good for your health.

DISCOVER IT YOURSELF!

Try this simple exercise routine to see how fit you are. Take your pulse before and after exercise. How long does it take your pulse to return to normal? As you repeat this routine each day, you should find that your recovery rate will be quicker and you will be less out of breath.

Athletes need to be very fit to perform well. They train hard for several hours each day.

1. To warm up, stretch your hands into the air and then bend at the waist to touch your toes five times. Bend over to each side five times.

2. Now start the exercises. Run in place for 15 seconds. Do three minutes of step-ups onto a bench. Then jump rope for two minutes.

3. Do 10 jumping jacks—legs apart and arms up as you jump, legs together and arms down as you land. Run in place for two minutes.

Index